Anonymous

Complimentary Banquet Given by the City Council of Boston to Rear-Admiral Lessoffsky

and the Officers of the Russian Fleet, at the Revere House, June 7, 1864

Anonymous

Complimentary Banquet Given by the City Council of Boston to Rear-Admiral Lessoffsky
and the Officers of the Russian Fleet, at the Revere House, June 7, 1864

ISBN/EAN: 9783337350697

Printed in Europe, USA, Canada, Australia, Japan

Cover: Foto ©ninafisch / pixelio.de

More available books at **www.hansebooks.com**

COMPLIMENTARY BANQUET

GIVEN BY THE

CITY COUNCIL OF BOSTON

TO

REAR-ADMIRAL LESSOFFSKY

AND THE

OFFICERS OF THE RUSSIAN FLEET,

AT THE REVERE HOUSE, JUNE 7, 1864.

BOSTON:

J. E. FARWELL & COMPANY, PRINTERS TO THE CITY,

37 CONGRESS STREET.

1864.

BANQUET

OFFICERS OF THE RUSSIAN FLEET.

MONG the formal entertainments tendered to Rear-Admiral Lessoffsky and the officers of the Russian Fleet, by His Honor the Mayor and the City Council of Boston, was a banquet at the Revere House, on the seventh of June. About two hundred gentlemen, including the members of the City Council, were present.

The Imperial Navy was represented by Rear-Admiral Lessoffsky, Captain Boutakoff, of the Flag Ship Osliaba, Captain Sarcovnin, Flag Captain, Captain Kremer of the Vitiaz, Lieutenant Lütke, Aide-de-Camp to the Grand Duke Constantine, Lieutenant Serebrakoff, Judge Advocate, and other officers.

Among the distinguished citizens invited to meet them were Hon. Edward Everett, Hon. Robert C. Winthrop, Admiral Stringham, commanding U. S. Navy Yard, at Charlestown, Hon. R. H. Dana, Jr., U. S. District Attorney, Prof. Louis Agassiz, of Harvard University, Hon. J. G. Palfrey, William Ropes, Esq., and his son Joseph S. Ropes, Esq., R. B. Storer, Esq., Russian Consul, and other foreign consuls.

The company entered the dining-hall at 6½ o'clock.

His Honor Mayor Lincoln presided, the Admiral occupying a seat on his right and Mr. Everett the one on his left. Rev. Dr. Hague invoked the Divine blessing. When the company had dined, the Mayor asked their attention, and said : —

" The first honors due on this occasion are to the Ruler of our Nation, and I ask you to rise and drink with me to

" The health of the President of the United States."

This toast was drunk with cheers, all rising, while the Germania Band, stationed in an ante-room, played " Hail Columbia."

The Mayor continued : " We were in hopes to have been honored with the presence of the Governor of our Commonwealth, but a domestic affliction has prevented his attendance ; I therefore would propose to you

" The health of His Excellency the Governor."

This toast was also drunk standing, the band playing " Hail to the Chief."

The Mayor then made the following remarks : —

GENTLEMEN OF THE CITY COUNCIL :

It is under no ordinary circumstances that we are assembled this evening around the festive board. The time and place, the state of our beloved country, the character and position of our distinguished guests, give to the occasion a significance and interest unexampled in our Municipal annals.

Our people are drawing near to the close of a desperate struggle, which is to determine the integrity of our National existence. At such a period we are assembled here in peace and quiet to entertain by becoming hospitalities the representatives of a foreign nation, whose sympathy has uniformly encouraged our efforts, and who will rejoice with us in the triumphal success of the cause to which we have given our best blood and treasure.

God, in his providence, has divided his children upon earth into many nations. To each He has assigned its peculiar and particular work. They do not become necessarily antagonistic on account of the difference of their geographical position, or the diversity of their political institutions; but their true fraternal relations to each other is discovered when one is suffering in adversity, and the other, with manly courage and unselfish devotion, seeks to cheer by its moral influence, and to show by outward demonstrations the strength of its friendship and the cordiality of its regard.

The great Empire of Russia, whose early history dates far back into the distant past, was one of the first to welcome our young Republic into the family of Nations. She has ever been frank and constant in all her intercourse with us. No bitterness or strife has ever caused any ill feeling; but from the commencement of our career until this day she has stood our firm friend and true ally.

The loyal people of the North, therefore, hailed with joy, last autumn, the arrival of his Imperial Majesty's Squadron in the United States. It did not bring arms or munitions of war to our assistance, — these we did not need, for with our own might we are bound to put down this Rebellion; but it brought more than these, ---

the kindly sentiment of International Brotherhood ; and it has given us the opportunity for the formation of those intimate personal relations with its accomplished officers, which will strengthen the ties already existing between the two Nations, and will have no inconsiderable influence in promoting the future prosperity of both countries.

Arriving first, appropriately, in the waters of the commercial metropolis of the Union, and there receiving the first shout of welcome from the people, then visiting Washington, our National Capital, and there cordially greeted by the President of the Nation, it finally honors us by its presence, and takes its departure from our Bay, after partaking of such farewell courtesies as it is in the power of our city to bestow.

The intelligent observer of events in the history of nations, can have no more interesting or inspiring theme of thought, than that furnished by the past career and future prospects of Russia and the United States. One a colossal Empire, its territory embracing in extent not only a large portion of Europe, but of Western Asia and America, and by its acts affecting the welfare and civilization of the Old World ; the other a youthful Republic, not yet hardened in its sinews, its powers and resources but half developed, but destined to be. the controlling influence in the affairs of the American Continent, and forming, on account of its maritime character, a power which will be felt in the old world as well as the new.

Diverse in their political organizations and their forms of government, they are both progressive nations, fostering, as time goes on, liberal sentiments, and each promoting by rational means the elevation of the great mass of the people. There is a contrast, and also a remarkable coincidence, in their history during the last three years. While one, by the will of its sovereign, and the approval of the most enlightened of his people, has peaceably emancipated and given freedom to twenty-two millions of his subjects, the other, although it knew it not at its commencement, has been engaged in a struggle which will accomplish, we trust, the same results for its own inhabitants held in bondage.

The present Emperor may have inherited titles and honors from his predecessors; but no act will render his name so famous in history, or cause his reign to be regarded with more grateful emotions by posterity than his proclamation of freedom to the serfs in his dominions. It will give him a title more illustrious than any of his predecessors, that of " The Liberator of his people."

We have a right, as friends of humanity, to congratulate him and his people on the new source of power which will be developed in his nation by this noble deed.

The compliment tendered to the United States by the friendly visit of the Russian Squadron is most heartily appreciated by the people of Boston. Its Municipal Government have, in various ways, sought to give an expression of the popular feeling. Our manufactories, schools, seminaries of learning, charitable and literary institutions, forts, arsenal, and navy yard, — our historical localities and public works, and everything which we believe would be of interest to the stranger, or give an insight into our national or social life, have been open to the inspection of its officers and men. And to-night we are assembled, in company with some of our own distinguished citizens, to pay to them and to the sovereign they represent our homage of respect and esteem.

I can assure you, Mr. Admiral, and Gentlemen of the Imperial Navy, that this assembly is convened for no idle purpose. The occasion may last for an hour, but the sentiment it represents is sincere and enduring. The friendship we have formed with yourselves has given a new interest to the country of which you are the honored representatives. Your flag has gracefully floated with our own at the masthead, and has mingled in the drapery of our festive occasions. It typifies that cordial good feeling and friendly interest which binds our two nations together.

In the presence of this assembly, and in the name

of the people of Boston, I tender you thanks for your visit. It has afforded the citizens of both nations an opportunity of knowing each other better, and of securing each other's regard. You have offered us your hand as a pledge of friendship in this day of our severest trial. We accept it; and may the God of Nations grant that in the future nothing may occur to cause its withdrawal, or to alienate the cordial relations now existing between the people of our respective nations.

I close, gentlemen, by proposing as a sentiment: —

"The health of their Imperial Majesties, the Emperor and Empress of Russia, and a cordial welcome to Rear-Admiral Lessoffsky and the officers of the Squadron under his command."

The band played the Russian National Hymn, and the company gave six cheers for Admiral Lessoffsky. He spoke in substance as follows: —

MR. MAYOR AND GENTLEMEN: I have been requested to say a few words. I am not a speaker, but I cannot say I am afraid to speak on this occasion, because I want to give vent to the feelings of gratitude which I feel, in common with my brother officers. This week, gentlemen, has been a week full of events, — I mean of events for our feelings. We have experienced your most cordial hospitality. We have been

2

introduced into those of your institutions where philanthropy soothes the sufferings of mankind. These are
most thrilling sensations. We have been introduced
into your schools, where you prepare citizens to be
your statesmen, — to be your defenders in the hours of
trial.

We have received so many tokens of friendship from
you, gentlemen, that I am convinced that the intelli-
gence will be hailed by you with feelings of pleasure,
when I tell you that since the hour when Emancipation was proclaimed by His Majesty the Emperor, not
less than four thousand schools have been established
by the people themselves. (Cheers.) A short time
ago, I regret to say, these men were but little more
than beasts of burden, but now, without any support
from government, they have made these four thousand schools.

Now, gentlemen, I cannot illustrate better the feeling
with which we are animated in gratitude to you than,
if you will allow me, by repeating a scene which I witnessed the day before yesterday, on board of my ship,
in New York — the Alexander Nevsky — which is
about to leave your country. The officers gave me a
dinner party. We were alone, our own family. There
was not a single American among us; but among the
toasts proposed, a prominent one, was a toast of gratitude to the Americans, and a wish for the prosperity

of their country. It was pronounced as it would be in any family.

The family there, gentlemen, was the officers who have experienced your hospitality and your good wishes, for which we are most grateful.

The Mayor then proposed the next regular sentiment, to which he called on Mr. Everett to respond. The toast was : —

Russia and the United States. As their territorial possessions together embrace the entire circuit of the globe, may the governments and peoples of the two countries ever be connected by the strongest ties of mutual friendship and good will.

Mr. Everett responded as follows : —

I obey your call, Mr. Mayor, with great cheerfulness, and I respond with all my heart to the toast which you have offered to the company. It is by no means an ordinary festival which has brought us together at this time, but, as you have justly stated, an occasion of unusual public significance and interest. I feel myself under obligations to Admiral Lessoffsky and the gentlemen of his suite and fleet, for a reason in some measure personal to myself. I had occasion, about a twelvemonth since, as a member of the Board of Visitors of the United States Naval Academy at Newport, in some remarks which I addressed to the officers and pupils of the institution, at the close of the examination, to speak of the importance of making provision for the instruction of our naval officers, not only in those scientific and technical branches and military exercises which belong to the profession, but in those broader studies, which pertain to a finished education, and I gave as a reason for this observation that the naval officer was often called upon to appear as the representative of his government in foreign countries. What more pleasing confirmation of the justice of this remark could I desire, than the agreeable impression which has been made upon our whole community, by the visit of our distinguished guests? Why, sir, a regular diplomatic agent, — an Envoy Extraordinary and Minister Plenipotentiary, may be received and treated with the utmost courtesy; he may discharge his duties with the greatest fidelity to his own government, — frankly and honorably toward the government to which he is accredited, but, after exchanging assurances of his highest consideration with the minister of foreign affairs every fortnight for a year, he will have done less to bring the people of the two countries together, than has been done by our amiable and distinguished guests in a week.

It has been the pleasing duty of the Trustees of the Public Library to do the honors of that institution to many distinguished visitors, foreign and native; among the former, to the youthful heir to the British crown, whose gracious affability and extreme propriety of con-

duct in a difficult position drew to himself a full share
of that respect and good will which the people of
America cherish, in a degree scarcely less than her
subjects, toward his royal mother, — and to the highly
accomplished and intelligent prince who stands in so
near a relation to the throne of France; but it is no
flattery to say, that the library has never, within my
knowledge, been visited by persons who have exhibited
a more enlightened and intelligent curiosity, as to the
nature, condition, and workings of such an institution,
than our respected guests.

Such are the fruits of a wise system of naval education; the education which has given to Russia such
names as Golovnin, Krusenstern, Lütke, Kotzebue,
and Bellingshausen; and which I mention quite as
much for the benefit of our own government and people, as out of compliment to our honored guests. It is
but about twenty years since our solitary naval school
was established, and it has by no means attained the
expansion required even by the ordinary wants of the
service. On the other hand, I find in a work of authority published several years ago, that there were
supported, under the minister of the marine in Russia,
nine naval schools of all kinds for the education of
officers, seamen, pilots, and engineers, in the Baltic
and Black seas, with an aggregate of more than two
hundred and fifty teachers and more than two thousand

five hundred pupils. You must, however, Admiral,
make some allowance for our youth. It is but a few
years — fifty at the outside — since the United States
claimed a place among the considerable naval powers ;
but it is more than one hundred and fifty years since
that most extraordinary personage, Peter the Great,
under the humble name of Peter Baas (Boss Peter)
wrought, with his own hands, in the shipyards of
Sardam.

   As you have truly remarked, sir, Russia was one of
the first powers to hold out the hand of fellowship to
us, on our appearance in the family of nations. Chief
Justice Dana of this State was sent as minister to Russia in 1780, and John Quincy Adams, then a lad of
fourteen, was appointed by Congress his private Secretary, the youngest person perhaps ever appointed to
such an office in this country. A pretty strong team
that, Mr. Mayor, Chief Justice Dana and John Quincy
Adams, and there are grandsons of those distinguished
personages in the hall, who show that the breed has
not degenerated. Mr. Harris, the British minister,
afterwards Lord Malmesbury, succeeded in preventing
the immediate recognition of Mr. Dana by the Empress
Catherine, but the moment it could be done without
offence to Great Britain, that is, as soon as the treaty
of 1783 was concluded, she recognized the infant
Republic with cordiality. From that time to this,

the best understanding has existed between the two governments. During the war of 1812 with England, Russia tendered her mediation between the two countries. It was not accepted by Great Britain; but the proposal resulted in a direct negotiation and the conclusion of the treaty of Ghent. For the whole period of our existence as a nation, the intercourse between the two governments has been most friendly. Never but in a single instance, and that more than forty years ago, has there been a difference of opinion leading to a discussion between them, and that yielded to an exchange of notes between Mr. Poletica and Mr. Adams.

When the late Emperor Nicholas resolved upon introducing railroads into his dominions, he sent a commission to this country to examine our public works of that description. This examination resulted in the engagement of Major Whistler (the engineer of our Western railroad) to superintend the construction of the railroad from St. Petersburg to Moscow. On occasion of the visit of the Emperor to London in 1844, I had the honor of being presented to him. A more magnificent figure of a man I never beheld; it was the youthful Hercules and Apollo moulded into one, and most like General Scott thirty years ago, and before age had laid its burden on his noble form. The Emperor spoke of Major Whistler in terms of the highest commendation. He said he was perfectly sat-

isfied with him in all respects ; and hoped he should
be able to retain him in Russia. On the premature
and lamented decease of Major Whistler, another
American engineer, Major Brown of the Erie Railroad was engaged by the Imperial government to com-
plete the road to Moscow.

In the last great struggle, in which Russia was in-
volved, the sympathies of the people of the United
States were, I think, generally with her. The causes
of the Crimean war were obscure ; and what we understood of them, to wit, a wish to preserve the integrity of the Ottoman Empire, did not appeal very
strongly to American feeling. We had no quarrel
with the Turks, but they were not objects of popular
sympathy. It was known, besides, to well-informed
persons, that the prime minister of England, Lord Ab-
erdeen, (one of the purest, wisest, and most honorable
men that ever governed England,) believed that the
war might have been, and consequently ought to have
been, avoided. His colleague, Sir James Graham, expressed the same opinion. The war was brought
about by the same agencies, wielded in part by the
same hands, which have been equally busy in the attempt to bring about a war between the United States
and Great Britain. I need not tell you that the duties
of an honest neutrality were faithfully performed by our
Government. Both of the belligerent parties procured

from this country, in the way of open trade, those supplies which the law of nations allows the neutral to furnish the belligerent; and in the solitary instance, in which an attempt was supposed to be making to build a ship of war for the Russian government, the remonstrances of Great Britain against this breach of neutrality were promptly and effectually listened to by the government of the United States.

But it is during our own tremendous struggle, that Russia has shown herself the wise, the firm, and the consistent friend of our country. Her Emperor and his enlightened counsellors saw, what France and England were slow to comprehend, that the rupture of the American Union would be an event as much to be deprecated by them, nay, by the slaveholding States themselves, as by our own constitutional Government. Never, I suppose, in the history of the civilized world has there been an attempted revolution, in which, — after the frenzy of the hour is passed, — success would be felt to be so signal a calamity by the revolting party itself, as it would inevitably prove to our rebellious States; and so entirely prejudicial to the best interests of the civilized world. This, however, was clearly seen from the outset by the Government of the Emperor of Russia. That Government alone of the three leading powers of Europe perceived, with prompt discernment, that the disintegration of the Union would

3 .

be disastrous to all parties, — a calamity to the family of nations, unrelieved by a single benefit. In that remarkable letter of Prince Gortschakoff, the Russian Minister for Foreign affairs, dated 10th July, 1861, and addressed to the Russian Envoy in this country, to be communicated to the Secretary of State, he uses this memorable language: "In spite of the diversity of their Constitutions and of their interests, perhaps even because of their diversity, Providence seems to urge the United States to draw closer the traditional bond, as *the basis* and *very condition* of their political existence. In any event, the sacrifices they might impose upon themselves to maintain it are not to be compared with those which dissolution would bring after it. United they perfect themselves; separated from each other they are paralyzed." And again, in the same remarkable despatch, Prince Gortschakoff, speaking in the name of the Emperor and of Russia, says: "The American Union is not merely, in our eyes, an element essential to the universal political equilibrium; it constitutes besides a nation, to which our august master and all Russia have pledged the most friendly interest; for the two countries placed at the extremities of the two worlds, both in the ascending period of their development, appear called to a natural community of interests and sympathies, of which they have already given mutual proofs to each other."

Words of sagacity and wisdom, as well as of friendship and peace! The Emperor of Russia tells the
American States, and tells them truly, that the Union
is the very condition of their political existence ; that
united they perfect themselves, that separated from
each other they are paralyzed. Such, in the opinion
of this impartial observer, is the Union. Does not the
slightest reflection justify the remark? Take first the
case of the States in rebellion. What would the doctrine of secession, if established, do. for them? It
would more than " paralyze," it would destroy their
political existence. It would place the territory of
the Confederacy, and all its relations with foreign
powers, at the mercy of each and every individual —
it might be disaffected — State. Texas, Louisiana,
Florida, recent acquisitions, all of them, from foreign
powers, might each and all set up for themselves ;
might fly off to France or Spain. Party spirit, domestic intrigue, foreign gold, the turn of a popular election, the will of a dominant faction might, on this doctrine, carry any one of them off to-morrow. In the
mean time, by the doctrine of secession, the entire Confederacy, considered as a whole, cuts itself off from a
great naval power of which it formed an integral part;
places its coasts, its ports, the mouths of its rivers at
the mercy of every maritime power, and this too at a
moment, when it defiantly announces that it has estab-

lished itself upon a corner-stone, which is daily rejected
more and more by the public sentiment of the civilized world.

But if the States in rebellion are guilty of this sui-
cidal frenzy, scarcely less at war with an enlightened
self-interest is the course which their sympathizers in
the leading maritime States of Europe have endeavored
to force upon the governments. What, for instance,
would be more against the interest of England, — the
country which it most concerns to enforce the duties of neutrals, — to establish the doctrine, that, in all
her future wars, and all future rebellions against her
central government, her antagonist, — it may be Canada, or Ireland, or Oude, or China, or New Zealand;
it may be a power that has not a seaport or a mile of
coast, — may put in requisition every shipyard and every
foundry in the neutral States, provided only the paltry
sham is observed of having the ships which are to
prey on her commerce built and equipped by one con-
tractor, and the armament furnished and sent abroad
by another, to be taken on board at a foreign port. Is
that a doctrine likely to benefit England in particular,
or the commercial world in general? or is it rather a
device by which private cupidity is enabled to break
down the barriers which for two centuries the law of
nations has been throwing round the rights and duties
of belligerents and of neutrals?

Again, after the Spanish colonies of this continent had asserted their independence of Spain, England importuned the United States to coöperate with her in preventing France from interfering to recolonize them; and when the United States yielded to her solicitations, Lord Brougham declared in the British Parliament that "no event had ever diffused greater joy, exultation, and gratitude over all the freemen of Europe than the language held with respect to Spanish America in the message of President Monroe to Congress." The Secretary and Biographer (Mr. Stapleton) of the British Minister labors to prove that the ground taken by the government of the United States on this occasion was suggested by that Minister (Mr. George Canning); and Sir James Mackintosh said, " I have already observed its coincidence with the declarations of England, which, indeed, is perfect, if allowance be made for the deeper, or at least more immediate interest, in the independence of South America, which near neighborhood gives to the United States. This coincidence of the two great English commonwealths (for so I delight to call them, — and I heartily pray that they may be forever united in the cause of justice and liberty), cannot be contemplated without the utmost pleasure by every enlightened citizen of the earth." What has England gained by a departure from this policy, and by acquiescing in the reduction

of Mexico to the condition of an Austrian colony under the protection of France? How much better,
with a view to her own traditionary policy, if she
could have perceived, with the Emperor of Russia,
that the perpetuity of the American Union is an element essential to the universal political equilibrium!

How much better for her own interests if France
could have perceived the same great truth! It has
been the policy of France, almost invariably pursued,
from the very dawn of our national existence, to promote the growth and prosperity of the United States,
as a counterpoise in the West of the maritime power
of England. This was alike the policy of the old
régime and the new _régime_. For this Louis XVI.
gave us arms, navies, and munitions of war; for this
the first Napoleon gave us Louisiana for a song; and
of all the errors in policy which his successor could
possibly commit, none can be imagined more at vari-
ance with the traditions and interests of France than
to do anything which will weaken the United States.
Regarding our Union, in the words of Prince Gortschakoff, as an element essential in the universal equilibrium, it would be just as wise in France to strip the
plates from her iron-clads, and leave their hulks to rot
at Brest and Toulon, as to assist in breaking up the
American Union into a group of small and fragmen-
tary States, exhausting each other in eternal border

wars, and compelled, from that cause, to abdicate their position as a great maritime power. So just and wise was the remark of Prince Gortschakoff that the American Union is an element essential to the *universal* political equilibrium.

Before I conclude, Mr. Mayor, let me make a remark which had almost escaped me. When our respected guests were at New York last year, receiving the attentions of the commercial metropolis, that portion of the English press which thinks the day lost, when it has not found some thing to abuse, or some person to vilify in the United States, was profoundly grieved at the honors paid to Russian officers, — "It showed such a want of sympathy for the poor oppressed Poles, on the part of the pretended friends of liberty!" Censorious people, Mr. Mayor, ought to have good memories. I am old enough to remember the acclamations of joy which burst forth in England when the armies of the First Napoleon, or rather the wretched fragments of his armies, were driven from Russia. There was a thrill of popular excitement which has never since been equalled. From every roaring cannon, from every pealing organ, from every human tongue, throughout the British Empire, arose one jubilant chorus of triumph. Well, sir, Alison tells us that for that terrible campaign, Poland furnished Napoleon 85,000 men. A fourth part,

certainly a fifth part, of that army over whose calam-
itous defeat all England was in raptures, was composed
of Poles. They fondly hoped that the Emperor of the
French was going to restore their independence, and
the bravest of their sons dyed the snows of Russia
with their blood. We were then fifty-one years
nearer the partition of Poland by Russia, Austria,
and Prussia than we are now, and the memory of
that transaction was proportionally fresher in the
minds of men. In 1813 it did not lead England to
reject the alliance with Russia; and if since that
period she has entered into the most intimate relations, political or personal, with those three powers,
I trust we may be forgiven, a half a century later,
for following their example.

Sir, the Emperor Alexander II. is not only a wise
and prudent, but he is a kind-hearted and benevolent
prince. By his autocratic word he has performed the
most magnificent act of practical philanthropy ever
achieved by a man of government. That he and his
brother sovereigns, the Emperor of Austria and the
King of Prussia, will attempt to undo the work of
Catherine the Second, Frederick the Great, and Maria
Theresa, by restoring the ancient kingdom of Poland,
nobody, I presume, expects or desires. If they did, it
would simply be the restoration of the worst government
in Christendom. That he will do all in his power to

improve the condition, promote the welfare, and elevate the character of his Polish subjects, may, I think, safely be anticipated of a sovereign, who, by the word of his mouth and from the impulses of his generous heart has spoken twenty-two millions of serfs into freemen and citizens.

I respond, therefore, Mr. Mayor, to your toast, with cordiality and emphasis. I recognize in the Russian Government a long tried, steady, and consistent friend; and I contemplate with patriotic pride this kindly tie, which, from the Atlantic to the Pacific, and from the Alleghanies to the Rocky Mountains, from the Rocky Mountains to Icy Cape, from Icy Cape to Kamschatka, from Kamschatka to Altai, from Altai to Ural, from Ural to Archangel and the utmost North, traversing the entire breadth of America, of Asia and Europe, (soon to be circled by the electric wire,) already unites the two great governments and peoples by the golden chain of friendship and peace. Never, never may the links be parted!

Mr. Everett closed with the following sentiment: —

The Navy of Russia, and a cordial welcome to its gallant and accomplished officers.

The toast was received with six cheers. Captain Boutakoff responded briefly, and closed with a sentiment complimentary to the American Navy.

4

The Mayor then alluded to the fact that the Congress of the United States being in session, no member of it was present on this occasion ; but said that he would call on a gentleman who had represented this city at Washington for a longer term than any one since the adoption of the Constitution.

The health of Hon. Robert C. Winthrop being thus proposed, the band gave the " Star-Spangled Banner." Mr. Winthrop's speech, which was heartily cheered at many points, was as follows : —

I thank you, Mr. Mayor, for the privilege of being present on this occasion, and of uniting with the City Council of Boston in these marks of respect for their distinguished guests. The speech of the evening is already made ; and made by him who is at once best entitled and most able to make it. But I cannot refuse to say a few words in response to your complimentary call.

As I look back on that long service in Congress to which you have alluded, I cannot forget the many kindnesses and courtesies for which I was indebted to the Russian Legation at Washington ; and I gladly avail myself of this opportunity, before alluding to any other topic, to pay a passing tribute to the memory of the late Mr. Bodisco, who for nearly twenty years, I believe, represented His Majesty the Emperor of Russia at our Republican Court. True always to his own country, he was yet animated with the same spirit which dictated that noble despatch of Prince Gortschakoff, to which Mr. Everett has so eloquently referred. He seemed to have the welfare and honor of our country, as well as his own, honestly at heart; to desire earnestly the preservation of our domestic peace and of our National Union; and to watch eagerly for opportunities of reconciling any antagonisms which threatened to disturb the relations of the North and South. Enjoying the intimacy and the confidence of our most distinguished men of all parties and sections, — of Clay and Webster, of Calhoun and Benton, and many others not unworthy to be named in the same connection, — he took peculiar pleasure in bringing them together beneath his own roof and around his own hospitable and sumptuous board, and in doing all that he could to soften the asperities and animosities which are too often engendered by the controversies of political parties and the rivalries of political leaders; and more than one personal difficulty, which might have led to most unhappy consequences, has owed its amicable adjustment to his timely and effective intervention.

I am happy to believe, Mr. Mayor, that a similar spirit has ever been evinced by the present Minister of the Russian Emperor, Mr. de Stoeckl, who was long associated with Mr. Bodisco as his principal Secretary, and upon whom his mantle has worthily fallen. Both of them, let me add, paid our country the compliment of taking to themselves American wives, — and very charming wives, too ; — and thus they had a right to feel that their relation to the United States was something more than one of mere diplomatic form and ceremony. I am sure, however, they were not induced to select American wives from any want of attractive and accomplished women in their own land. I have seen, indeed, but few Russian ladies. The only one, I believe, whom I have ever met on American soil, is the wife of the distinguished officer at my side, who may be called, after the phrase of Shakespeare, " our gallant Admiral's Admiral ; " — whom we have all seen here with so much pleasure, and who will be accompanied by our best wishes on her embarkation in the steamer for Europe to morrow. But I have another in my mind's eye at this moment, whom I have been privileged to know in another land, — she is now no more, and I may not presume to pronounce her name on any public or festive occasion, — but whose varied and brilliant accomplishments, whose familiarity with almost every language spoken beneath the sun, whose graces of manner and charms of conversation and kindness of heart, and, above all, whose fortitude and heroism under the deepest personal and physical suffering, will never be effaced from my remembrance.

I do not forget, Mr. Mayor, the many estimable and excellent representatives of other lands whom I have had the good fortune to meet at the capital of our country; but Mr. Everett I am sure will agree with me, that no Legation has been more uniformly or more highly valued and respected than the Russian Legation, personally and officially, by all who have been privileged to know those who have composed it. I regret that M. de Stoeckl could not have been with us to-day, that we might have included him in the compliments of this occasion, and that we might have united in drinking his health, with all the honors to which he is entitled, as the accredited Representative of the Emperor.

The Russian Empire, sir, has been less visited by American travellers than any other of the great countries of the old world. It has always seemed a great deal farther off from us than other countries, and in many other respects besides physical distance. Its institutions are in the greatest possible contrast to our own. Its domestic policy in years past has often been the very reverse of that which we could all have wished. Its names are very hard to pronounce, and even harder to remember. Its language is very difficult to be learned, and is understood by so few of us, that we have been obliged to take all our accounts of the land and its inhabitants at second hand. As a matter of geography, indeed, we have not failed to observe its magnificent distances and colossal pro-

portions on the map. As a matter of history, we have
not omitted to recognize the giant strides with which it
has marched on, and is still marching on, to no second
place among the nations of the world. But practically, and as a matter of personal concern, it has
rarely been recalled to us by any thing more substan-
tial than the Nesselrode pudding or the Charlotte
Russe on our bills of fare ; by the hemp required for
the rigging of our men-of-war, or for the smaller rope
which is sometimes brought into uncomfortable play in
cases of treason or of crime ; or,— more agreeably, certainly than either,— by the glorious Hymn now known
to all our orchestras, and adopted in all our churches,
which is by no means inferior even to the far-famed
anthem of Old England in the richness of its harmony,
and the majestic grandeur of its cadences. But recent
events have changed the whole aspect of our relations
with Russia. The Emperor's late noble act of emancipation at home, and his kind and generous words con-
veyed in the despatch of Prince Gortschakoff to our
own Government, have struck a sympathetic and re-
sponsive chord in every American breast, as directly
and as effectively, as if those magnetic wires which
Mr. Everett has just foreshadowed, and which are even
now in preparation, had already been stretched across
the Siberian desert, had already been strung along the
banks of the Amoor, had already vibrated over Behr-

ings Straits, and as if the living spark had leaped at
a bound from the palace of the Czars to the hearts of
the American people.

And now, while we are welcoming the Russian flag
and the Russian fleet to our harbors, and exchanging
these acts of courtesy with so many intelligent and
gallant officers of the Imperial Navy, let us not forget
the health of the General Admiral of that navy.

It was my good fortune, seventeen or eighteen years
ago, to see this distinguished person in London. He
was then a very young man, and he had come over,
not in disguise, like Peter the Great, but openly and
avowedly to study the military institutions and naval
establishments of England. I saw him reviewing the
Queen's household troops in company with the late
lamented Prince Consort and the ever honored and
illustrious Duke of Wellington, and I was afterwards
privileged to meet him at the British Court. We have
an Aide-de-Camp of his with us on this occasion, —
himself the son of the President of the Imperial Academy of Sciences, and whose voice has already been
welcomed at the opening of our new Hall of Natural
History.

I propose the health of His Imperial Highness the
Grand Duke Constantine, the General Admiral of the
Russian Navy.

The toast having been received with cheers, and the band having played the Russian Hymn again, Lieut. Lütke, who had been referred to by Mr. Winthrop as Aide-de-Camp to the Grand Duke, responded in the name of his illustrious chief. He said —

Mr. Mayor :   I must say — having been in the closest intercourse with the Grand Duke — I know his ideas in reference to the American nation, and that, being one of the Princes of the Imperial blood who has been an active member of the Government, that the Prince has been, in the great act of the Emperor, a most active member, and was one of the committee to carry out the act of emancipation. I am sure that the Grand Duke has a most hearty feeling for America, and for her progress, for he is himself a man of progress. He has heard of all the improvements which you have made in the different kinds of manufactures, and has sent out to America men to study these improvements. Amongst others whom he has sent, I take the liberty of mentioning Admiral Lessoffsky as being sent to examine your iron-clad ships and monitors. It is the Grand Duke who has put the navy on its present footing, and introduced the monitors into our navy. I am sure that he will be very glad to have heard his name pronounced in this distinguished society, and I thank you in his name for the honor Mr. Winthrop has done him.

The Mayor announced the next toast : —

" *The Admiralty and Maritime Courts of Russia and the United States.* May they never adjudicate in questions of prize upon American or Russian vessels."

RICHARD H. DANA, JR., ESQ., was called upon to respond. He said : —

MR. MAYOR : Adjudication upon prizes, though it may have a judicial sound, means WAR ; and war between Russia and the United States of America I take to be as improbable as anything in human affairs. If nearly a century of harmony and good offices indicates anything, or furnishes any security for future peace, we have the fullest assurances here.

When we were in the struggle for our independence, to throw off the rule of a distant government in which we had no voice or hand, which claimed an unlimited jurisdiction over us and all we had, we sent to Russia a citizen of Massachusetts (to whom you, sir, and Mr. Everett, have kindly alluded in connection with my name) ; and, although she gave us no fleet or army, we got from her a moral support, which did much — those familiar with that history know how much — toward securing, at last, the recognition of our independence. This, sir, was a good beginning ; and circumstances made sure for years a fair following of the beginning. In that dark period of wars the world around, when neutrals were in danger of being

5

crushed between the giant belligerents at sea, Russia and the United States had a common interest, and were kept in sympathy and co-operation on the great questions of belligerent and neutral rights. It was not only the fear of the mistress of the sea that oppressed neutral commerce. There was almost as much danger from coercion, in ports on the Continent, by the feebler maritime power of France. Thus, neutrals were threatened if they did not co-operate with the weaker, or submit to the law of the stronger. In that partial eclipse of peace and commerce that covered so long the habitable globe, Russia and the United States together strove for the light of peace and the beneficence of commercial intercourse.

But, sir, Russia has not only maintained peace with us, but has kindly and wisely done her best to keep us at peace with the world. When the war of 1812 was upon us, she offered, as Mr. Everett has reminded us, her mediation. She did not ask the contending parties to abide her decision as an arbiter, or to allow of her intervention. She asked them only to receive her advice as a mediator. We accepted the offer at once, and empowered our ministers to act upon it. Great Britain refused it, and the war was fought out to its end. I hope she had good reasons for the refusal; but Sir James Mackintosh did not think so, and censured the refusal in terms of strong condemnation.

Again, the treaty of 1782 had left open a question of compensation for property — including slaves, I regret to say — on territory which England was to restore to us. To whom did we go for arbitration? Why, to Russia, most naturally; and the arbitration of Russia, made, and repeated on new questions arising out of the first decision, was satisfactory. But there was one question between us, of such magnitude and difficulty that neither of the Treaties — that of Paris, in 1782, nor that of Ghent, in 1814 — seemed able to close it, — that was the Northern Boundary. Nearly the whole line, from the Island of Grand Menan, off Eastport, to the Lake of the Woods, was in dispute. Such was our confidence in Russia, that we were ready to put all our rights and interests on that vast issue in her hands. England objected to the arbitration of Russia, and we fell back upon the unlucky King of the Netherlands, whose " Dutch highlands," lying in the beds of rivers, left the question open, with all its elements of irritation, until it was closed by the great act of three men, capable of large ideas and high action, — Peel, Webster, and Ashburton, in 1842.

This is not all, sir. Our day of distress, weakness, and peril came upon us. We met with sad disappointment in the tone of speech from friendly nations. They told us, by the speeches of statesmen and the voice of the press, that we had grown too strong, and that we must expect them to wish for our division. Some, more civilly, assured us it was for our good to be divided. " Rise and be hanged, Master Barnardine! These are your friends, the hangmen, Master Barnardine!" I hope we may forget, no doubt we should try to forget, the ill-concealed delight with which our misfortunes were witnessed, as well as the open derision, obloquy, that was poured upon us in those days : the utmost efforts made to secure against us the opinion of the world on every available ground. And when the commander of a sloop of war, uninstructed, does an act, the legality of which the law officers of the British Crown and the British press first admitted and then questioned, without waiting to learn whether our Government sustained or repudiated it, the British Government, which, in any other state of this country would have unquestionably made it matter of diplomatic inquiry, availed themselves of the occasion to make a military and naval demonstration against our blockade and entire war, — for that I take to have been the plain English of the *war movement* in the Trent affair.

From this trying picture, how pleasing it is to turn to the aspect which Russia presented to us. Mr. Everett has read to us the friendly and graceful message of Russia to America sent to us in our darkest hour, — telling us that the preservation of our

Union was essential to the universal political equilibrium, and that Russia stood pledged to the most
friendly interest. Well did Mr. Seward, in reply, acknowledge that the friendship of Russia " had its beginning with the national existence of the United States."
I must return, Mr Mayor, to the subject to which
you more immediately directed my attention, the prize
courts and navy of Russia. Of its courts, I cannot
speak from personal knowledge ; but of its navy, it
has been my fortune to know something. I have met
Russian ships of war in all quarters of the globe. At
the Sandwich Islands, they told me with delight of the
escape of the frigate Diana from a British fleet which
came to Honolulu, in 1854, a few days after the Diana
hurried away ; — that same frigate whose singular
fate, a few months afterwards, attracted the attention
of the scientific world, lifted up from her anchors
in Simoda Bay, in Japan, and swamped by one mon-
strous swell of the sea, in a quiet day, which rolled
from Japan to California, with the regularity of the
march of a planet, raising and plunging everything in
its course, until its last effects were registered by the
astonished watchers of the tide gauges at San Diego
and San Francisco ; — and when I was mentioning
this, just now, to the Russian officer whom I have the
pleasure of finding at my side, he replied, — " O yes !
our Admiral commanded the Diana then." I met them

in China, in Japan, and I found a squadron at San Francisco; and when I went to the navy yard at Mare Island, in California, there I found a room full of Russian naval officers who had been examining our works. Wherever science, or general knowledge, or national interests called them, there Russian ships of war were found. And, our friends will not think me indelicate or assuming if I pay my tribute to the high order of education I always found among them. All spoke French, — and the world knows that Russian French is the best out of Paris, — and most spoke English also; and it is well known that among Russian naval officers are found competent representatives of their country in diplomacy and science as well as war.

Let me ask your leave, sir, to propose, not as a formal toast, — that is not my office, — but as a sentiment to be taken into our hearts: *The friendship of Russia and America, beginning with our national existence, in our darkest hour showing no abatement, may it last as long as there shall be Russia in the old world and United States in the new.*

At the invitation of the Mayor, Captain Kremer, of the Vitiaz, responded to this sentiment, speaking substantially as follows: —

Mr. Mayor, — I hope you do not expect a very handsome speech, but since I am called upon I can speak only what is in my heart. I take it as a fact, proved and confirmed this night by so many remarkable orators, that Russia has a very warm sympathy in the United States ; and I know, also, that Russia as well as the United States at this moment depends upon her army. You have had severe trials, and you have them at this moment. I know many people in Europe are surprised that you are progressing so slowly towards Richmond, but I know, having been in Sebastopol, how to appreciate your difficulties. Perhaps you may hear to-morrow that Richmond is taken. But whether it is taken to-morrow or after to-morrow, I have no doubt it will be taken very soon. I have the honor to propose a toast — " The Army of the United States."

The Mayor gave the following : —

" *The Army of the United States.* In the past our pride ; to-day our steadfast hope."

Lieut.-Col. D. F. Jones, 11th Regiment, U. S. Infantry, responded briefly.

The next sentiment was : —

" *The Navy of the United States.* The iron as well as the wooden walls of our country."

Rear-Admiral Stringham responded, and concluded with the following : —

Russia — The great Empire of the North : *The United States* — The great Republic of the North : May they con-

tinue to be true to each other until the compass forgets to
point to the pole.

The Mayor then gave the following sentiment, and called
upon Prof. Agassiz to respond : —

" The man of Science, — a citizen of every country. Are
we Americans? so is he; are they Russians? so is he. With
us he has always a home."

Prof. Agassiz said : —

Mr. Mayor: A naturalist is at ease when called
upon to do honor to the Russian navy; for that branch
of the service of the Empire has a splendid record in
its connection with the progress of the natural sciences.
Scarcely had the great expedition which added continents to the world known to the ancients, come to a
close, when, in the competition for contributions to all
the departments of science, the Russian navy took
a most prominent part.   In this century, especially,
there is only one among the many expeditions sent
out by the governments of Europe, which had the
start of the cruise of Admiral Krüsenstern around the
world, the results of which contributed to the progress
of every branch of physical science.   But as a Zoolo-
gist, I am particularly reminded of the great importance of the contributions to Natural History of the
two expeditions around the world, commanded by
Capt. Kotzebue. · To it we are indebted for Esch-
scholtz's unsurpassed works on Acalephs, and to the

remarkable facts concerning alternate generations observed by Chamisso. Passing over the other expeditions which had more direct bearing on geographical discovery, I cannot forget that Admiral Lütke's voyage was one of the most important in the annals of physical science for the comprehensiveness of the investigations conducted by its gallant commander, now President of the Academy of Sciences in St. Petersburg. But even the misfortunes of the Russian navy have turned to good account for science. When the ship Diana, commanded by the Admiral whom we have the honor to-day to welcome as our guest, was wrecked on the coast of Japan, it sent to our coast the most important scientific message that ever crossed the Pacific. The earthquake wave that shook it to pieces sent us word that the depth of the ocean, on the line from Simoda to San Diego, is fifteen thousand feet.

Well may we, therefore, congratulate ourselves upon the loss then sustained; and, instead of regretting it, Admiral Lessoffsky may remember with satisfaction that his name is forever connected with the first measurement of the depth of the Pacific Ocean.

At this point the Mayor remarked that, as a pleasant episode in the exercises of the occasion, he had the pleasure to present to Admiral Lessoffsky an elegantly bound volume, containing a

6

reprint of a paper published in the Boston Courier, in 1855, in
defence of the policy of Russia during the Crimean war, entitled
" A defence of Russia by an American."

The Mayor also stated that the book was printed for presentation by the writer of the paper, and was a magnificent speci-
men of the typographic art.

On receiving the gift, the Admiral said : —

MR. MAYOR, — This present cannot be too highly
valued, and I regret to say that I am little used to
speaking in public, and cannot express, as I would
like, my feelings of gratitude for the honor I have
received. I only say this to correct an error; not an
error, but something which is not in this book. I
mean a photograph of the banquet which is to be
given to-morrow to our junior brothers, the sailors.
Wherever hospitalities have been shown us in different countries, I do not recollect a single one where
the junior brothers have been regarded, and it is to
the philanthropy of the Commonwealth of Massachusetts that the Russian sailors owe this most grati-
fying event.

The name of the author of the work was repeatedly called
for by the company, and the Mayor announced Franklin W.
Smith, Esq., a merchant of Boston.

Mr. Smith, on rising to acknowledge the calls of the company, briefly stated the circumstances under which he had been
led to prepare the work just presented ; remarking that, when
nine years since, his ardent sympathy and interest in behalf of
Russia, against the allied powers, incited him to the expression

of his opinions through the public press, nothing was farther
from his expectations than that they would be reproduced and
published on such an occasion as the present; and also that the
Mayor would bear witness that this public presentation of the
volume was not according to the writer's intention, but at His
Honor's request.

After alluding to the extraordinary advance of Russia, Mr.
Smith stated that a few weeks since he had been informed that
there was in this country an extraordinary document, a ukase of
His Majesty Alexander II. Fortunately, he had been able to
obtain a written copy during the afternoon, in time for the
present occasion. It established precedents, under law and
authority, that would abide to her honor in the annals of Russia;
and would be welcomed by the future historian as worthy to fol-
low an edict that gave freedom to twenty-two million of serfs.

Directly it concerned the personal interests of two humble
individuals, — the smith, Jamshon, and the tailor, Gaertner,
of the town of Goldingen; but as directly, also, it recognized
and promulgated the great principles of religious toleration, for
an Empire.

We may well rejoice, said Mr. Smith, in the increasing evi-
dence of the wonderful progress of Russia, — material, educational, political, and religious, — under the government of His
Imperial Majesty Alexander II., Autocrat of all the Russias.

The Mayor then gave the sentiment, —

" *The Merchants of America engaged in the Russian trade.*
To whom we are indebted in no small degree for the cordial
feeling which unites the two nations."

Joseph S. Ropes, Esq. responded as follows : —

I cannot refuse, sir, to respond to a call addressed
to Russia merchants ; yet the genial and friendly so-

ciety into which I have been thrown during the last week, carries me back far beyond my mercantile experience, and makes me desire to speak rather as the graduate of a Russian university. My own place of education was but a stone's throw distant from that of my friend the Admiral, and I have near me, not classmates indeed, but successors in the institution which I am proud to call my *alma mater*.

A thoughtful mind can hardly fail to notice the parallel which suggests itself (indeed it has already been alluded to) between the two nations here represented. We call a continent our inheritance; but Russia stands between *two* continents, of both whose destinies she may one day be the arbitress. Like us she has vast prairies, broad inland seas, rivers that water half a continent, mountains abounding in wealth of iron and copper, silver and gold; vast material resources, the development of which will one day astonish the world. Even her errors and misfortunes have their parallel in our own; and her experience is in some respects the prophecy of our future.

But the most striking and interesting point of comparison between us has been already and most eloquently dwelt upon. We have all heard of Peter the Great, whose resolute energy transformed the face of an empire. But there was one obstacle before which even his iron will was forced to recoil, — the national *beard*, which typified the ignorance, stupidity, and superstition of the Russian peasant. He could shave his army, his navy, his nobility ; but his peasantry he could not shave. In other words, he could not raise them to the level of civilized and educated humanity.

Alexander the First attempted emancipation, and failed. Nicholas made one experiment and immediately abandoned it. Alexander the Second *has accomplished it !* Future history will record the noble magnanimity, the indefatigable perseverance, the indomitable energy, and the steadfast resolution by which that great work, the greatest as it seems to me of this or of any age, has been successfully completed.

On one of the, vast squares of St. Petersburg stands a magnificent column, bearing a colossal bronze statue, and dedicated, as its inscription tells us, by " grateful Russia to Alexander the First." But in the hearts of thirty millions of emancipated peasants, Alexander the Second has laid the foundations of a monument more enduring than that bronze, —, a pyramid more lofty than the royal and imperial palace which it overshadows, — one which the frosts and storms of northern winter can never injure, and to which time will but add new strength and beauty.

And here, sir, I might fitly pause ; but the knowledge that many ears near me which would gladly hear the praises of their noble monarch, cannot

readily appreciate them in a foreign tongue, induces
me, in accordance with your kind invitation, to en-
deavor, in my poor way, to express to them some-
what of our feelings on this occasion.

The following remarks were made in the Russian language : —

GENTLEMEN OF RUSSIA, OUR HONORED GUESTS : —
Permit me, an American, yet for you not a foreigner,
to express to you the esteem and present the sincere
and hearty greetings, not only of the City of Boston,·
but of the whole American people. Returning to
your homes, bring to your countrymen the assurance
that Americans have not forgotten, and never will
forget, the ancient and steadfast friendship, shown
them by the sovereigns and the people of Russia.
Fifty years ago, we heard of Alexander the First as
the deliverer of Europe from a heavy political yoke;
but in Alexander the Second we have found the
benefactor of mankind, bestowing personal liberty,
domestic happiness, and civil rights on thirty millions of people. " Grateful Russia to Alexander the
First," has raised amidst her capital a noble monument; but Alexander the Second will be celebrated
with eternal praise by *grateful humanity*.

The Mayor then gave, —

" *Emancipation in Russia*. The noblest work of Imperial
Justice."

Hon. J. G. Palfrey responded, and concluded by giving a sentiment of perpetual peace between Russia and the United States.

Lieut. Col. John Q. Adams, Aide-de-camp of his Excellency the Governor, was introduced by the Mayor as one of the grandsons alluded to by Mr. Everett.

Col. Adams spoke as commissioned, he said, by his Excellency, of the bond of friendship between the two countries, growing out of the emancipation of the Russian serfs and the American slaves.

Rev. William Hague, D. D. was next introduced. He responded briefly for "The Clergy."

In response to a call from the Mayor, Hon. George S. Hale, President of the Common Council, made the following remarks : —

I cannot but be grateful, sir, for the accident of my official position, which induces you to call upon me as the representative of one branch of the City Government, and gives me an opportunity to join in expressing in their behalf the hearty and cordial welcome we are here to give to our distinguished guests — the representatives of a great and friendly power, who gave us so early and so kind a welcome into the family of nations, whose cordiality has been so constant in prosperity, whose sympathy so ready in our adversity. I know there are many who are surprised at these cordial relations between nations whose institutions are apparently so diverse. But I have learned also that those who have studied them more closely find the explanation easy. The greatest empire and the great-

est republic, the mightiest autocrat and the most pow-
erful democracy, balance the political scales of the
world, — what wonder that they look upon each other
with interest? In Russia, as in America, different
races, — " Parthians, and Medes, and Elamites, and the
dwellers in Mesopotamia," — as it were, are rapidly
forming one homogeneous nation, entitled by all intel-
lectual and physical laws to an inheritance of vigorous
intellects in strong bodies.

I do not think it is altogether fanciful to suppose that
the physical peculiarities of the two countries may tend
to assimilate the nations that inhabit them. In each,
vast territories, mighty rivers, and inland seas, varied
climates and abundant wealth, on land, in the seas,
and in the bowels of the earth, stimulate the same
restless ambition, the same vastness of purpose, the
same eagerness in the pursuit of wealth and freedom in its expenditure. I read that, twenty-five years
ago, the present Emperor of the French — a witness
not too partial to either — declared that he could then
" perceive only two governments which properly fulfil
their providential mission, — the two colossi at the end
of the world, — one at the extremity of the new, the
other of the old." Each, he said — " the one guided
by a single will, the other by liberty " — was charged
with the noble office of winning to civilization the vast
territories which lay before their open grasp. And

under the influence of these causes their tendencies in some respects are singularly coincident. The tendency in Russia to-day is, to free the slave; to raise the masses; to spread education among them; to render them independent by assuring to them an interest in the soil ; to diminish the power of the privileged classes; to increase that of the law, and to improve its administration.

What wonder if two nations sympathize with each other, one of whom turns with just pride to the memory of its greatest Sovereign, that " Pieter Timmerman," the shipwright at Saardam, who " rose early, boiled his own pot, and received wages for his labor; " while the other welcomes and recalls to its highest post one who hardened his hand with early toil, and accepts as the political cry of an election the appellation which proclaims such an origin ? What wonder if America, in its eager race westward and southward, has sometimes paused to watch with interest the giant strides of Russia over new lands and seas. It is said, sir, that " the Yankee farmer and the Russian peasant are the only rustic people on the face of the earth who are capable of holding town meetings, and who do so instinctively and practically." And, in language whose accuracy I will not assume to judge, but which might well apply to ourselves, they are described as restless, fond of emigration, hospitable and lavish, eager in the pursuit of wealth, but not tenacious in retaining it.

7

"What is decided by the community," says their proverb, "must come to pass, — the will of the people is the will of God."

Shall not a community like ours, with educational institutions, in which it takes a just pride, feel a warm and earnest sympathy with those serfs of whom our distinguished guest has spoken; who, within two years, since freedom was fully theirs, have established four thousand schools at their own expense? And, while I am speaking of educational institutions, pardon me if I allude to two local coincidences which cannot but have some interest for us at this moment.

That admirable instrument, the telescope at Cambridge, which we had the pleasure of exhibiting to our guests a few days since, is the twin sister of another of similar worth, which adorns the Russian observatory at Pulkowa, wrought by the same cunning hand. Hardly does that cease to count the stars, when this takes up the wondrous tale, — and the rising sun bears to us a greeting from those whom his declining rays there invite to their nightly labors.

That other instrument, also, which to-morrow will seek to give another welcome, in tones more dulcet and harmonious than the *vox humana* to-night — the Great Organ at the Music Hall — is the work of the same artist who constructed, nearly thirty years ago, a similar instrument for St. Peter's Church at St. Petersburg, unequalled by any other in the Empire, as this is the finest in the Republic.

It is a singular and pleasing application of the sentiment of Louis Napoleon already quoted, that there, an imperial decree "guided by a single will," recognized the claims of art in remitting the duties upon the organ of St. Peter's Church, while here, Liberty, expressed by law, admitted our own, in the same way, as a work of art.

But, above all, sir, what wonder that we, who, after so many years of political strife, and now, through I dare not count how many tears, how much agony and what rivers of blood, hope at last to reach the liberation of four millions of men, to whom we are bound by the tie of a common humanity? — what wonder that we should turn with admiration, with sympathy, with respect and affection, to the man, be he emperor or autocrat, who has lifted into the pure air of freedom, by measures full of wise and apprehensive caution, over twenty-two millions of men of the same race and blood, and to the nation who have sustained his undertaking with disinterested patriotism; and who seem both to recognize that sentiment so familiar to us in the often quoted words of the most mellifluous of English poets, —

"Princes and Lords may flourish or may fade,
A breath can make them, as a breath has made;

> But a bold peasantry their country's pride,
> When once destroyed can never be supplied," —

and aim to secure to their country this foundation.
I wish, sir, that I could borrow the knowledge, the
memory, and the silver tongue of the distinguished
gentleman by your side to whom we have listened with
so much pleasure this evening, that I might recount
the early instances of Russian courtesy, and the signi-
ficant and frequent cordialities of her sovereigns. We
all remember the philosophic and statesmanlike letter
in which Prince Gortschakoff expressed the sympathy
of his august master, and,

> " Last of all, an admiral came ; "

not, in the humorous words of the English poet, —

> " A terrible man, with a terrible name,"

but an accomplished and cultivated gentleman, of supe-
rior intellect, abundant knowledge, quick and careful
observation, and ready appreciation, familiar with men
and the world, like that Homeric sailor, and bearing
a name which we shall long remember with high regard. Russia seems to us to-day, as our great poet of
creation writes, like the

> " Lion pawing to get free
> His hinder parts," ready to spring, " as broke from bonds."

While those, I think, who have studied her progress, and the spirit which is rising there, look forward with hope to the hour when liberal institutions shall spread —

> " Where, through the sand of morning land,
>   The camel bears the spice ;
> Where fur-clad hunters wander
>   Amid the northern ice,"

and Europe become in a nobler sense both Republican and Cossack.

Mr. Mayor, the feast is ended. The wine is poured. You have given to me the office of fulfilling the Homeric maxim, which bids us to —

> " Welcome the coming, speed the parting guest."

And I pray our friends, for such we claim them now, to bear to their homes, on a happy and prosperous voyage, the cordial greeting of the Republic to the Empire.

MUSICAL FESTIVAL.

FESTIVAL.

On the eighth of June the officers of the Russian Fleet attended a Festival at Music Hall, given in their honor, by twelve hundred pupils of the Public Schools of the city. The following programme was successfully carried out.

I.

SONG OF WELCOME.

Air — RUSSIAN NATIONAL HYMN.

Sea-birds of Muscovy, rest in our waters,
  Fold your white wings by our rock-girdled shore ;
While with glad voices its sons and its daughters,
  Welcome the friends ye have wafted us o'er.

Sea-kings of Neva, our hearts throb your greeting!
  Deep as the anchors your frigates let fall,
Down to the fount where our life-pulse is beating,
  Sink the kind accents you bear to us all.

Fires of the North, in eternal communion,
  Blend your broad flashes with evening's bright star !
God bless the Empire that loves the great Union ;
  Strength to her people! Long life to the Czar !

To be followed by "HAIL COLUMBIA."

II.

TRIO.

From " Elijah " . . . . . . MENDELSSOHN.

Sung by the pupils of the Girls' High and Normal School.

8

III.

CHORAL.

"Let all men Praise the Lord " . . . . MENDELSSOHN.

IV.

SELECTIONS FOR THE GREAT ORGAN.

BY MR. B. J. LANG.

V.

PRAYER FROM DER FREISCHUTZ.

IN MUTED TONES.

VON WEBER.

VI.

GLORIA IN EXCELSIS.

From the "Twelfth Mass " . . . . . . MOZART.

VII.

THE OLD HUNDREDTH PSALM.

From all that dwell below the skies
Let the Creator's praise arise;
Let the Redeemer's name be sung,
Through every land, by every tongue.

Eternal are thy mercies, Lord;
Eternal truth attends thy word;
Thy praise shall sound from shore to shore,
Till suns shall rise and set no more.

.

www.ingramcontent.com/pod-product-compliance
Lightning Source LLC
Chambersburg PA
CBHW031751090426
42739CB00008B/959